CH008733335

OPEN to Be
INSPIRED and WILLING
to Be an INSPIRATION

SANDRA GARDNER

BALBOA.
PRESS
A DIVISION OF HAY HOUSE

Copyright © 2019 Sandra Gardner.

Interior Image Credit: Sandra Gardner

All rights reserved. No part of this book may be used or reproduced by any means, graphic, electronic, or mechanical, including photocopying, recording, taping or by any information storage retrieval system without the written permission of the author except in the case of brief quotations embodied in critical articles and reviews.

This book is a work of non-fiction. Unless otherwise noted, the author and the publisher make no explicit guarantees as to the accuracy of the information contained in this book and in some cases, names of people and places have been altered to protect their privacy.

Scriptures taken from the Holy Bible, New International Version®, NIV®. Copyright © 1973, 1978, 1984, 2011 by Biblica, Inc.™ Used by permission of Zondervan. All rights reserved worldwide. www.zondervan.com The "NIV" and "New International Version" are trademarks registered in the United States Patent and Trademark Office by Biblica, Inc.™

Balboa Press books may be ordered through booksellers or by contacting:

Balboa Press
A Division of Hay House
1663 Liberty Drive
Bloomington, IN 47403
www.balboapress.com
1 (877) 407-4847

Because of the dynamic nature of the Internet, any web addresses or links contained in this book may have changed since publication and may no longer be valid. The views expressed in this work are solely those of the author and do not necessarily reflect the views of the publisher, and the publisher hereby disclaims any responsibility for them.

The author of this book does not dispense medical advice or prescribe the use of any technique as a form of treatment for physical, emotional, or medical problems without the advice of a physician, either directly or indirectly. The intent of the author is only to offer information of a general nature to help you in your quest for emotional and spiritual well-being. In the event you use any of the information in this book for yourself, which is your constitutional right, the author and the publisher assume no responsibility for your actions.

Any people depicted in stock imagery provided by Getty Images are models, and such images are being used for illustrative purposes only.
Certain stock imagery © Getty Images.

Print information available on the last page.

ISBN: 978-1-9822-2485-1 (sc)
ISBN: 978-1-9822-2487-5 (hc)
ISBN: 978-1-9822-2486-8 (e)

Library of Congress Control Number: 2019903692

Balboa Press rev. date: 03/30/2019

CONTENTS

INTRODUCTION

What is your purpose? We all have a purpose to fulfill. It may come to us unexpectedly or come at the right time in our lives. There are times when you have set backs or challenges that will call your attention to your purpose. Your purpose in life defines who you are as an individual. Our existence here on earth is for a reason.

<u>Open to be Inspired and Willing to be an Inspiration </u>is a book of inspirational quotes that will guide you to realizing that life is a journey that will lead you to your purpose. The messages are based on the power to produce effective results within you. So, sit back and relax or join others in a discussion on discovering your purpose in life.

LOVE

Dear friends, let us love one another, for love comes from God. Everyone who loves has been born of God and knows God. Whoever does not love does not know God, because God is love.

1 John 4:7-8 NIV

Love is the special unconditional gift that God has afforded us with. When the presence of that gift is acknowledged, that is when the acts of human kindness flourishes to an existence of brotherly and sisterly love honoring the adoration of the love of God.

Family is the cornerstone of strength and love; it's that strong knitted vessel that runs deep through our souls, it's like a covenant, a teaching of love and morality that is given to the successors, the cornerstone of love.

Love indeed nourishes our whole being. Love is the oxygen that travels through our blood stream and is released among the atmosphere. Love is inhaling God's evergreen without any persecution. Love is life.

Be of good cheer is acknowledging God's everlasting love.

Follow God's path by being in the most suitable existence on planet Earth.

The remarkable you will be jelled amongst the greatest.

Sandra Gardner

Pitch black darkness will zoom erratically in your presence when a variation of God's gift or change needs to take its form.

The arm that was extended far and beyond shouldn't be forgotten.

Sandra Gardner

You're a total gem that needs to be treasured forever with an everlasting impression of endurance, dedication, and unconditional love.

Be grateful for the small things in life, treasure its most valuable worth.

Sandra Gardner

To be a contributor of charity is to acknowledge and spread God's love.

A strong honorable dedication of a career of love that will last until eternity, with God being the lead and in control during those awakening midnight hours challenging you to handle life's positions that occurs during inopportune times. Gods has chosen your career as an amazing being based on nurturing love.

Follow that golden path that God has amazingly paved for you.

God anoints us with a grand gift that encourages, helps, entertains, and inspires others.

Sandra Gardner

When times are uncertain, God will strengthen your total being and He will never forsake you.

God walked and talked with us and carried our hearts in His hand to help us accomplish an amazing life.

Jump start the bandwagon to advertise the creator's abilities.

Our God will diminish anger and fear when His charitable love is received and acknowledged through His power.

The half awaken glow rise of the incredible Earth centers the attraction of a new day is born.

Birds chirp to serenade love in admiration of a comforting extraordinary bold glow of life that sets the bountifulness of a graceful horizon.

Sandra Gardner

A smile will never be forgotten, it's a remembrance of a beautiful spirit that God has graced.

Positivity will adorn the heart rather than attack the heart.

God is the creator of inner beauty and that is joy.

Peace is the key of a loving life that God grants you.

Sandra Gardner

Every awaken moment is a communion of surrender to God for casting His powerful abilities in the destructive hours of dismay.

You are giving this beaming glorious day of life so that your gift of compassionate spirit exercises love.

Life lessons, journeys through life, rigorous pace of life, gives a glowing light of comfort when the grandest gift of love is treasured as gold.

Embrace your mind on the gift because the outcome is grand.

Sandra Gardner

Have the audacity to extend God's natural warmth that's planted in your soul to start recovery.

Admire yourself, you are the unique essential entity that makes up your being.

Being grateful doesn't have a price, it is simply gratitude.

Prayer is the ultimate comforter. Prayer is victorious, the dolce can overcome any obstacle.

INSPIRATIONAL

Have I not commanded you? Be strong and courageous. Do not be terrified; do not be discouraged, for the Lord your God will be with you wherever you go.

Joshua 1:9 NIV

How do we derive to a place of hope? We become inspired by others' obstacles to triumph and through our experiences in life. However, having a reason to have hope is to seek for a change. When that time is needed, there will be a sense of urgency, a need to be courageous without doubts of fear. It is awesome to be in that rim in life; we're able to learn from our mistakes and teach lessons from them.

Having faith in God and believe that the impossible is possible with His strength, guidance, and protection all things are certain.

Sandra Gardner

Acquire knowledge is to build a foundation for success by exploiting your potentiality to the best of your ability.

Be the brave honorable soldier that shares the soul, without one is of nonexistence.

Cherish God the best way possible so that life can be fulfilled abundantly.

The leaders of the new school follow and be instructed by the strong.

Ask God for strength to overcome an obstacle, remember faith comes first.

Don't take life for granted because you will miss the joy of life.

Sandra Gardner

The joyous guiding light will lead you to a sun beaming life that you want to be a part of instead of a life you have to fulfill.

God will neutralize your anxieties by accepting His comforting love of peacefulness.

The morning sun will rise brightly, I hope your inner being is shining as lovely as the magnificent sun.

Adversity is a reassignment of life that sparks a new beginning.

God whirlwinds you through some devastating surroundings to get to better days.

Adversity is a life lesson, it elevates us to become what we are intended to be and where we need to go in life.

Fear doesn't flat line us; it rises us to the occasion to get it accomplished.

Bread will crumble when the most significant ingredient is outcasted as the missing link.

Sandra Gardner

Don't pass judgement on the crisp pristine unseal envelope allow the tethered implanted document to surface in passing.

A clean bill of health is a step in the right direction toward a resolution.

Sandra Gardner

Continue to blaze the trail, the dazzling radiant neon glare is impeccable.

Assert shamelessly for sufficient help so that recovery could manifest.

Sandra Gardner

The amazing life will capture the dancing eye and that circumstance will lead you to become a conqueror.

Don't be complacent in a mediocre mindset of just idling by because God has something in store for us to adore.

Yourself will be marveled as somebody, if you think you're marvelous.

You are your best friend so trust yourself.

When something is allowed, it is accepted.

Love can change everything even the unconsciousness of a soul.

Life is going to revolve in motion and take care of itself.

God answers prayers when options are diminished.

Predecessors are the successors' future; the predecessors determine how the outcome will unfold.

The precious joy that you possess will be cherished forever.

Sandra Gardner

Being the victim in the trenches will teach you how to be in the opposition of becoming a victor.

Transform the foul pessimistic mess into a powerful restorative message to be an affirmative living testament that will be a favor for doubters or downers to rejoice.

An unyielding sense of purpose wins the race all the time.

Indulge in the delightfulness of God's grace and guidance with a humble attitude of gratitude.

God announces His charitable love to you through the natural beautiful creation of life, this is His life of love.

Going out on faith and being covered with God's protection is awesome.

God is forever spreading His everlasting love that creates the spirit of God; therefore, it is shared and cherished as a keepsake.

Weathering the storm dazzles the optimistic thought of positivity that one will seek to grasp conditional love.

God will repair your soul when you allow Him to do his will.

Always open your humble heart to extend your hands as comforter to others.

A dark smokie discomforting cloud can enter your path and create a bold lit array of humbleness that will make challenges become mellow.

There is a reason, season, or a situation for every incomprehensible circumstance that encounters our lives; however, there is a strong endearing message regarding the circumstance that the vulnerable will cling onto and most likely rise!

Don't escalate the volume of the bark to overpower the content and validity of your position or stance.

All hands-on deck is a phrase of endearment that gives presence to the honor of unification is beautification as hearts link amicably to a path of sisterly and brotherly love.

This is a glorious day of refuge and peace in His holy name.

The courageous soul shall never be in vain.

Sandra Gardner

Open to be inspired and willing to be an inspiration.

Lead and challenge the doubtful bewilder to an astonishing refuge of peace and tranquility.

Growth and wisdom create a new beginning. It is like a rebirth of shedding dead skin from the mind. We are constantly evolving socially, knowledgeably, and spiritually to advocate our greatest gift that God has bestowed upon us.

A descending screaming wave will cascade on a disparaging rocky stream of emotions or agitates a content boulder.

God will lead you in the right direction.

Faith prevails when there's direct contact on demand which causes a matter to be lifted.

Sandra Gardner

Outer flare exemplifies perception but the inner being explicates the realization of you.

Don't ever think things are impossible because of a few bumpy roads, the sun rises daily in reference of a new beginning.

We should be balanced to deal with the comings and goings in our spaces.

God creates the spirit of love, it is the anchor of smooth sailing.

Sandra Gardner

The day before will never be seen in our existence, but the presence of tomorrow will soar bravely like an eagle.

God created our uniquely being so that we could implement our special abilities to capture this phenomenal world.

Sandra Gardner

The powerful fuel of endurance has us to react courageously bold in an uncompromising setting.

Don't underestimate your abilities, be the shine or gift that you are granted.

CARING

He guides the humble in what is right and teaches them his way.

Psalms 25:9 NIV

Caring illustrates an open heart to share to others that are in need. The initiative of kindness is asserted when people are not able to care for themselves due to sickness, being elderly, living in anguish, or turmoil. As we navigate through our life, we observe what is important and how we could be of service of rescuing lives.

Being kind soothes the heart and makes loving simple.

Sandra Gardner

Allow your lovely gestures of amazement to over shadow misconceptions of preconceived notions.

The scripture teaches us to execute our efforts kindly, humbly, lovingly toward mankind.

Sandra Gardner

God has blessed you to be the first to smile at someone, a friendly gesture is very worthy.

Accentuate care by genuinely acknowledging despair to mold and repair.

Embrace boastfully a positively radiant image and sincerely bless an unsettled heart with your spark.

Afloat the troubled waters of demise by lending hand.

Sandra Gardner

Showing courtesy is that inner being of humbleness nature that eases tensely circumstances.

MOTIVATIONAL

I can do everything through him who gives me strength.

Philippians 4:13 NIV

We all have the desire to achieve or make a goal attainable. There has to be a strong willingness to go outside your comfort zone to make that happen. Most of the time we have to go out on faith. Faith is having that strong belief of being fearless. When our faith has been formed and shaped to inner strength, there is no returns only moving forward. Our inner strength, God, and positive individuals will help us in attaining the goals we long to desire.

Verbiage dictates emotions while settling suggests nonchalance.

Sandra Gardner

A mission is not impossible as far as the appropriate tools, strategic thinking, and firm techniques are implemented.

To be commemorated as a respecter, self is at the highest esteem.

Sandra Gardner

Continue to carry the torch of education, it is establishing an ambitious life.

God knows your ability; therefore, He will enable you to get it done.

Sandra Gardner

Continue to be the insightful griot that deliver messages throughout a life span to enlighten generations.

Education is power that will boost you to countless avenues.

Brighten your delightful world with an array filled with a sunny spirit that will flaunt a calming disposition.

Be the gift of gab to lighten a day.

Sandra Gardner

Moving forward means to accept the cause by being able to handle the ripple effect.

An adventurer will capture what is best creatively and excel with it.

Sandra Gardner

The mesmerizing big picture of a situation or goal is quiet pleasing to the observers' eye.

A strong balance in life neutralizes anxieties and makes life fearless and fierce.

Sandra Gardner

Release your spirit and dance to the beat of your drum because you are well verse with that vibrant tune.

Create the atmosphere with warmth it's very necessary.

Sandra Gardner

Strike the blazing wire to an amazing sparkling glow when the wire is ready to be gallantly exploited.

Awesomeness, courageousness, and encouragement is building a unit of success.

Create your world with amazingly talented individuals that complement you.

PEACE

Peace I leave with you; my peace I give you. I do not give to you as the world gives. Do not let your hearts be troubled and do not be afraid.

John 14:27 NIV

Does it appear sometimes that it is difficult to live in peace? Happiness equates a peaceful mind. In order for us to derive to that place of tranquility, we have to free ourselves from the disturbances that plague our environment. Living in peace requires a positive mindset of thinking and living peacefully of ignoring distraction that echoes madness. It can be acquired by alleviating chaotic stressors that causes the disturbances within us by surrounding ourselves in calming spaces.

Forgiveness is creating an inner peace of comfort so that we challenge those unfortunate souls that constantly echoes disruption.

Sandra Gardner

Don't leach boldly to negatively that will be reciprocated because it is wasteful energy.

Peacefulness relaxes the anxiety of a chaotic soul.

Sandra Gardner

The Lord will shelter your burden neatly when your habitat is steered with strife.

Create a harmonious bond that an implicated rocky ship will not sink.

Sandra Gardner

Acknowledge joy in the Lord magnifies an uplifting spirit.

God's creation of the Earth is a caption that depicts the beautification gloriously and the peacefulness of the natural elements that fulfills the Earth's surface.

Surround your establishment in an unflustered atmosphere that enhances a safe haven of comfort that will catapult the driving force to a peaceful nature of humanity.

A sacred day of delivering calmness, prayer, restoration, and meditation to sanctify the body of cleanliness.

Sandra Gardner

Travel through life with happy baggage and thoughts that will enhance a peaceful inner spirit.

The flimsy whimsical dancing and crisp singing of the brutal leaves on the most magnificent trees that sing sweet harmonizing verses of peace, as they stood out in the breezy wind to be marveled for grace.

Sandra Gardner

The beautiful captivating blue sky that surrounds and energizes lives with a bright sunny array of spirits that bows in the shadowy surface underneath the green breezy trees of meditation.

Take life as an adventure don't raise the anxiety, capture situations calmly.

Sandra Gardner

You are the chosen one to lead and inspire the doubtful bewilder to an astonishing refuge of peace and tranquility.

Don't debate yesterday, compromise today to have a more unified tomorrow.

Peace is what one needs in the heart to extend God's grandest treasure which is love.

Do not stir the boiling potion when the mixtures are already filled with strife, let it simmer to ease the pain.

When the disparaging times desperately seeks chaos, go to that hiding place of refuge to absorb, meditate, and release God's loving energy.

HAPPINESS

Nehemiah said, "Go and enjoy choice food and sweet drinks, and send some to those who have nothing prepared. This day is sacred to our Lord. Do not grieve, for joy of the Lord is your strength."

Nehemiah 8:10 NIV

How can happiness exist in our daily lives? Your life is in your hands. You have the choice to be pessimistic or optimistic. When you are doing the most for others, blessings will certainly flow from God in your favor. It is so essential to be in the company of positivity because that energy will flourish making life less complex. Remember, it is possible to be happy. We carry that possibility with us daily.

The most rewarding experience is helping people that need you the most.

Sandra Gardner

Increase visibility of self-respect by being the best you.

You are that tool that's needed so your light can beam internally and outwardly.

God will repair your soul when you allow Him to do His will.

Take a moment to remember it is not all about that person, you are that person.

Adjust your life as you see fit.

Administer a grain of salt to the discomforting annoyance.

Sandra Gardner

Unlock the royal treasures of the heart to rescue that poignant gem.

Engage in the heroic fever of a dancing heart.

Sandra Gardner

Represent your lovely gestures of amazement so the inner being could explosively ignite like sparkling colorful fireworks.

Standing in confidence is God's way of declaring His powerful strength, through all things you shall prosper.

The electrifying positive energy will reciprocate genuinely.

The soul is the spirit of God that energizes the ability to extend comfort, caring, peace, and love to the shattered and non-shattered souls.

Sandra Gardner

Groove into socially conscious music that illuminates the spirit of awareness and appreciation.

The endearing connected souls of the kindred spirit sparks a dance of joy to what matters.

Sandra Gardner

Positive energy will explode a colorful warmth of vibrant love that's recognizable.

When your intentions are geared toward positivity, the positive spirit of a being will dance its way to your soul.

ENCOURAGEMENT

So do not fear, for I am with you; do not be dismayed, for I am your God. I will strengthen you and help you; I will uphold you with my righteous right hand.

Isaiah 41:10

When we hear the chattering voices of others, that is when we allow supporters to be our cheerleaders. Create an abundance of hope and never giving up on what we believe we can accomplish in our hearts. To be encouraged is giving affirmation in building your confidence for success. Remember, you are not walking alone in the challenge it is with those cheerleaders.

Be diligent in your efforts to reach your destination.

Effort is effective, it's worth a million.

Don't underestimate your abilities that God has bestowed upon you.

Sandra Gardner

The Lord gives us endurance to react courageously bold in an uncompromising setting.

Don't let the company of anger applaud your spirit rather let it feel unwelcome.

The remarkable you will be jelled amongst the greatest.

Pay adequate attention to your needs so that you can live a life of pleasure and longevity.

Sandra Gardner

I wasn't the little girl that threw stones; I used them to build.

Don't wait for it to happen attack it before it happens.

Sandra Gardner

Safe guard your heart with a steel protective suit of armor to deactivate the undesirable forces.

Don't let the majority rule, you are the ruler.

Sandra Gardner

The robustness of determination soars vigorously without any limitations.

Don't decapitate the message just listen.

Be about the action rather than complaining about the action.

If there is no action, that's null and void.

Sandra Gardner

Our predecessors have enormously strong shoulders, don't fret because their spirit will keep you grounded with firm balance.

Be the inspiring orator that carries the millennial generation through a path of no limitations.

Join the incredible fight of the Women's Empowerment Movement to be a role model of efficacy.

Keep the faith strong so that God's brand could be leaked out through the spirit.

Take precisive, precautionary, progressive measures in wavering options before representing as a selector.

This is your time to chase your calling.

Believing in God and know all things are possible, then the conqueror mode is set forth.

During the tidal waves of disparaging emotions, the rocky boat rocks vigorously, it is life calamities which leads to strength.

Yesterday is forever in the atmospheric wind that is enchanted with a hint of glimmer, glitzy, gloomy. Atmospheric wind is a learning experience that will guide the appropriated path.

Don't hold onto negativity because it is wasteful energy.

Sandra Gardner

The ambitious will travel the celestial stratosphere without a doubt full of exploration, admiration, and confidence.

Be the encouraging motivator that sets the tone of being an effective role model.

Encouragement is not a form of weaponry of battle; it is that extraordinary soaring force of knowing that the sky is the limit.

When you approach uncomfortable situations, don't feel less than demonstrate confident assertiveness.

Be patient with time, life has valuable opportunities for explorations.

RESPONSIBILITY

Whatever you have learned or received or heard from me, or seen in me put it into practice. And the God of peace will be with you.

Philippians 4:9 NIV

We hold ourselves accountable for people or things we have control over; however, it is our responsibility to be dutiful in our dealings so that learned behavior can be demonstrated in a positive light. If we are leading the next generation, we have to set the tone by showing what we know. They will practice it and follow the learned behavior.

Be determined by the courageously strong audience that flatters dignity so that their contributions will not diminish as obsolete.

Sandra Gardner

Learning is an essential component to success that has no color barriers.

Information showcases a wealth of knowledge that is platformed with a variety of venues.

Sandra Gardner

Parents lead, converse mutually, demonstrate, mold, and nurture.

Be an effective adviser, it speaks volumes; however, an ineffective adviser whispers incompliance.

Exercise your talent to electrify souls.

Assert knowledge, life is valuable.

Sandra Gardner

Continue to be the beckon of life that is structured architecturally to a statuesque view of adornment.

Have a highly up standing desire to demonstrate self-respect not falter it.

Always live up to your gift because it is God's acknowledgement of your value here on planet Earth.

Education and knowledge are empowerments that will ascend to the next dimension.

You learn, live, love those experiences will most likely heighten the degree of your endeavors.

Stand astutely with confidence in honor of courageousness to support the challenge of bravery.

Sandra Gardner

A day of decluttering the mind, body, and spirit with a detoxification of fast, meditation, and prayer.

Soul search your ambition as it lies within your compassionate heart like a flickering soaring eagle that is about to capture the attention of adoring bystanders.

The wiser stand courageously strong with a bravery stance in a prideful morality status to represent ordinance and discipline so that the successors could live and lead by example.

Growth comes from experiencing life which leads to the real.

Sandra Gardner

Creativity, inquiry, exploration, and information generates knowledge.

Be an impressive expeditor so excellence can out weight defeat, weigh in on the challenge heavily on prayer, meditation, wellness, fitness to conquer and keep the repetitiveness of stamina and endurance alive.

Sandra Gardner

PERSEVERANCE

He replied, "Because you have so little faith. I tell you the truth, if you have faith as small as a mustard seed, you can say to this mountain, 'Move from here to there' and it will move. Nothing will be impossible for you."

Matthew 17:20

God is fighting your conflicts organizing things in your best interest even though you see it as impossible. When we grab hold on the steadfastness of completing a task, it is faith that guides us through accomplishing our goals. Sometimes we have doubts and feel that our possibilities are limited or minimized. Most importantly we must remember that God conquers our worries in a less strenuous approach.

A struggle is a fight towards reaching your destination.

Having a plethora of strength is what one needs to conquer the unimaginable while being diligent in his or her efforts so that success can prevail.

The acquired motivation is needed to leap over any default as long as you focus on the direction, drive, and put your best accelerated foot forward.

Focus on being the best you! There will be minor components that complicates or compliments the well-being. The major focus is the goal; therefore, you shall exploit your major focus to your capacity. Remember, it is about being the best you!

Life will throw you curve balls in many directions; the point is that you have to be ready to catch them.

Sandra Gardner

Professionalism, audacity, progressiveness, proactive, persistency can accomplish tasks without a doubt.

The grayish tethered wounded broken fence has weathered the storm of erosion; however, that old ragged fence will stand astutely arm and arm with mended fences to acknowledge that the storms will be defeated.

There is a thin line and that line has to be balanced very delicately so that lion's roar won't captivate.

Education nourishes the brain and energizes the mind.

Rise to the occasion of justice, the truth will reveal its face when a stance of integrity, order, just in dealings, and boldness occurs towards a stone face.

Force the unfortunate stone wall by elevating stamina to maximum capacity so that endurance will promote possibilities.

Sandra Gardner

Change is hard, but success is gratifying.

SCRIPTURE INDEX

OLD TESTAMENT

Joshua
1:9 NIV
Nehemiah
8:10 NIV
Psalms
25:9 NIV
Isaiah
41:10 NIV

NEW TESTAMENT

Matthew
17:20 NIV
John
14:27 NIV
Philippians
4:9...13 NIV
1 John
4:7-8